SELF-DISCIPLINE MASTER

How To Use Habits, Routines, Willpower and Mental Toughness To Get Things Done, Boost Your Performance, Focus, Productivity, and Achieve Your Goals

KEVIN GARNETT

ERRORS

Please contact us if you find any errors.

We have taken every effort to ensure the quality and correctness of this book. However, after going over the book draft time and again, we sometimes don't see the forest for the trees anymore.

If you notice any errors, we would really appreciate it if you could contact us directly before taking any other action. This allows us to quickly fix it.

Errors: errors@semsoli.com

REVIEWS

Reviews and feedback help improve this book and the author.

If you enjoy this book, we would greatly appreciate it if you were able to take a few moments to share your opinion and post a review on Amazon.

ENQUIRIES & FEEDBACK

For any general feedback about the book, please feel free to contact us at this email address: **contact@semsoli.com**

Table of Contents

INTRODUCTION

How would you like to have financial freedom?

Are you feeling stuck, wishing you'd have more free time?

Is it possible to become a **Self-Discipline MASTER?**

There is a way.

But you may be surprised to learn how you can experience more freedom...

To experience more freedom in your life, you need more of the opposite: <u>self-discipline</u>.

That may sound paradoxical, allow me to explain. If you want:

- more free time, you will need to get better at time management.

- financial freedom, you need to implement financial discipline now, with a long-term focus.
- to be healthy, free to go out and do as you please, you need to eat healthy and exercise regularly.

By being disciplined in how you use your time and resources, you can create the life you always wanted!

What You Will Learn

That is easier said than done though, isn't it? You and I are not robots, and temptations are waiting around every corner.

You made an excellent decision picking up a copy of this book. Already, you stand out from most other people because you are taking action.

And I highly respect that. You won't be disappointed!

This no-fluff guide will help you to develop self-discipline. You will learn:

- how to develop goals
- plan out a course of pursuing those goals

- be accountable

- overcome temptations, as well as

- deal with possible failures along the way

And that is just the tip of the iceberg.

Action Steps

Also, this book is very practical. When you bought this book, you weren't looking for a 2,000 pages boring academic treaty on every theoretical aspect of self-discipline. Am I right?

You are reading this book for one reason only: to get stuff done!

In yoga, there's a famous saying: 'An ounce of practice is worth more than a ton of theory'. The same goes for self-discipline. Your life is not going to change by just reading this book. The real change comes when you *apply* what you learn.

That is why every chapter ends with **Action Steps**. These small exercises serve two purposes. They:

- allow you to **reflect** on what you just learned

- encourage you to **take action**

So, I hope you are excited!

I am really happy to have you on board.

We have a lot to talk about. Let's get started, shall we?

Kevin Garnett

CHAPTER 1: WHAT IS SELF-DISCIPLINE, AND WHY SHOULD YOU CARE?

"We all have dreams. But in order to make dreams into reality, it takes an awful lot of determination, dedication, self-discipline, and effort."

Jesse Owens

Key Takeaway: *Self-discipline is the way we practice certain good habits and stay away from certain bad habits in order to live a happier life. It is very applicable in the modern age and will help you overcome things like procrastination as it replaces your need for instant gratification with looking forward to the better delayed gratification.*

In an age of instant gratification and indulgence, many believe that self-discipline is a lost art. We think we are doomed to procrastinate and never achieve our goals. Some are coming around to the idea that self-discipline is something that can positively turn their lives around. Perhaps you are one such person. Maybe you want to be:

- an entrepreneur,
- an Olympic athlete, or
- a mother who can rally her children around her in an orderly fashion,

Or maybe you want to:

- learn how not to procrastinate, or
- just feel less out of control in emotions or finances.

Whatever the case may be, you picked up this book for a reason: to learn about self-discipline and how to implement it in your life.

What is Self-Discipline?

When we think of someone who practices self-discipline, we often envision someone who maintains a great level of self-control over their physical, spiritual, financial, or social life.

For example, we think of:

- military personnel who exercise to keep up their physical capabilities,
- East-Asian monks who deny themselves food and water to be able to meditate,
- the wealthy who saved up every penny to become rich, or
- CIA agents who keep a great level of secrecy concerning their identity and work.

When we define self-discipline in this way, we do ourselves a disservice, making a disciplined lifestyle and mindset out to be unattainable. While self-discipline includes some self-denial, also known as asceticism when taken to the extreme, it is not limited to simply keeping yourself from pleasures and desires!

Let's start then, by redefining **self-discipline** as:

- *practicing certain **positive habits**, and*
- *refraining from certain **negative habits**, in order to*
- *improve your **state of living** and **interactions** with your environment.*

Some examples of positive self-discipline include exercise, prayer, financial budgeting, planning for time management, and practicing a skill like playing an instrument or writing. Examples of self-discipline that negates an activity are fasting, dieting, stopping smoking or drinking, breaking an addiction, and even just stopping habits like biting one's nails.

What does a disciplined person look like, then?

A person who practices self-discipline does not have to be someone who trains for an Olympic sport, who commits to life as an international spy, or who lives an entirely vegan lifestyle. A self-disciplined person can simply be a person who cuts out coupons for grocery shopping (not just extreme couponing either), a person who reads their Bible on a daily basis, a person who attends a weekly support group meeting, a person who replaces soft drinks with water in their diet, or a person who commits any large or small task and *follows through.*

But Everyone's Doing It!

The thing about self-discipline is: everyone does it, just not everyone does it well.

Another way of thinking about self-discipline is to see it as a way of managing goals that are in conflict with each other. For example, you might encounter a situation in which you really want to sleep but you need to get up for work. In this situation, the conflicting goals are sleeping in and keeping your job. You must choose which of these goals matters more to you in the moment and in the long run, and discipline will enable you to stop hitting the snooze button so you can crawl out from under the warm covers into the shower and get on with your day.

The Stanford Marshmallow Experiment: Self-Discipline Is The Key To Success

Self-discipline is also about delayed gratification in place of instant gratification. If you are set on obtaining satisfaction instantaneously, you might be at odds with your long-term happiness. In the previous example, if you go back to sleep every morning and show up to work hours late, if at all, you will lose your job.

In the short run, you might gain a few hours of rest, but in the long run, your comfort of having a place to work to pay for a place to live and sleep is at stake. In most cases, instant gratification puts something more vital to your existence in danger than the short-term desire you perceive as needing to be satisfied.

This is perfectly illustrated by the now famous Stanford Marshmallow experiment.

In the 1960s, a team at Stanford University conducted experiments where they tested hundreds of young children, around 4-5 years old. Each child would be brought into a room, alone. This was just a basic room, with a table and a chair. The child would be asked to sit on the chair. Next, a marshmallow would be placed in front of him.

At this point, the researcher says something along the lines of: *"I have to go outside now for a while. If you do not eat this marshmallow while I'm away, I will give you a second marshmallow* when I return and you can eat them both! But you won't get the second one if you eat this one before I'm back."

Then, the researcher left the room for 15 minutes, while the team observed what the child did.

You can imagine it must have been pretty funny to watch. I would have loved to be a member of that team! Seeing those kids struggle. The marshmallow is *right there*. But if I don't eat it, I get two...Maybe I should sniff it? Yes, I can do that. Lick it? I can still get my second one if I do that...

TIP: This test has been replicated many times. You can see some really funny videos on YouTube of kids fixated on the marshmallow, fighting an inner battle: to eat or to wait and get two?

In the end, most kids gave in. However, a few children were able to wait until the researcher returned to the room.

The cool thing about this experiment is that they kept track – for decades! – of how these children performed later on in life. And what did they find? The kids that waited for the second marshmallow, or in other words: who were willing to delay gratification, ended up:

- scoring higher on SAT tests
- responding better to stress
- having a lower chance of becoming obese
- having lower levels of substance abuse
- having better social skills (according to their parents)

Basically, they simply scored better in life.

The lesson from the Marshmallow Experiment is that, in order to be successful long-term, you will need be disciplined. Delayed gratification over instant gratification.

So, self-discipline not only protects you from failure like losing your job but also promotes success, helping you rise within the ranks of your company to greater responsibilities and prestige. As U.S. President and explorer Theodore Roosevelt said, *"With self-discipline most anything is possible."*

This does not mean you can fly or even become the King or Queen of England by sheer discipline and willpower, but it does mean that you can reach your full potential and function in a satisfied, fulfilling lifestyle if you are willing to exercise self-control and persistence.

Self-Discipline Equals Freedom

Jocko Willink, who was a Navy SEAL for 20 years, explains it best in Tim Ferris's' book *Tribe of Mentors*: Discipline equals freedom. We all want freedom. Financial freedom, mental freedom, more free time. But how do we get it?

We already touched on this in the Introduction of this book: through the *opposite* of freedom, self-discipline.

- Want more free time? Then apply time management and be disciplined in your work
- Want financial freedom? Don't go out for dinner three times a week. Instead, implement financial discipline now, with a long-term focus.

The term time management is somewhat misleading. The concept of time is fixed, so you can't really manage it. But you can manage yourself. By being disciplined in how you use your time and resources, you can create the life you always wanted!

Action Steps

1. How do you define self-discipline?
2. In what areas do you demonstrate good self-discipline?
3. In what areas are you lacking self-discipline?
4. Mimic the Marshmallow experiment. Buy something sweet you really like. Put it in front of you, as you sit quietly in a room. Don't touch it. Instead, imagine being 4 years old again. What is going through your head? Can you delay the gratification of eating that yumminess that's staring you in the face?

CHAPTER 2: WHO NEEDS SELF-DISCIPLINE

"True mastery transcends any particular art. It stems from mastery of oneself--the ability, developed through self-discipline, to be calm, fully aware, and completely in tune with oneself and the surroundings. Then, and only then, can a person know himself."

Bruce Lee

Key Takeaway*: Everyone needs self-discipline. It is part of what makes us happy in life and helps us attain our dreams.*

Bruce Lee, famous in both the film and the martial arts world, wisely spoke that self-discipline spans a wide variety of arts and practices and focuses on the *knowing* and *mastering* of yourself.

Some books will focus on discipline needed to stick to a diet or exercise program, and this is a noble endeavor to be sure, but it is not the only aspect of our lives in which self-discipline is helpful and even necessary. Just to give you an idea of how this book might impact various parts of your life, I want to take a minute to look at what self-discipline looks like in those areas. That is, I want to ask: who uses and needs self-discipline?

The Physically Fit and Healthy

As I mentioned before, those desiring to be physically healthy in terms of eating and exercise habits require self-discipline. If you want to implement a certain exercise or eating regimen in your life, you must be able to commit to research, know, and abide by certain guidelines that the regimen prescribes.

- If you go low-carb, for example, you will need self-discipline to stay away from breads and pastas and eat vegetables and meats instead.
- If you are looking to implement a certain exercise routine, you must commit to blocking out the time in your schedule for the routine and to doing the exercises that are part of that routine.

These might seem self-explanatory, but it would be a shame to exclude this in our discussion of self-discipline.

The Financially Stable and Growing in Wealth

Those who desire to create financial stability for themselves and grow their financial resources also require self-discipline. They must practice restraint. They cannot buy every single thing that catches their eye.

If you seek to grow your wealth, you cannot indulge your every whim. Why? Because whims are expensive and will cost you the funds you hope to save and possibly invest in more lucrative endeavors.

Financial success will cost you in the short run but will literally buy you what you want in the long run, and therefore it requires self-denial temporarily to help you achieve your long-term goal.

The Religious and Spiritually Active

Religions and spirituality cost us time, as well as mental / emotional / spiritual energy, though they often return more than they have taken. For example, if we are willing to give up food and water for the daylight hours of the month of Ramadan, Muslims believe we are able to gain much more spiritually than we give up physically.

Fasting is common to virtually all religions, in fact, and makes clear that self-discipline is a trade-off of what we forego for what we gain by a practice, act, or payment. Prayer, for example, costs time, but often promises communion with a deity as a return on your investment. Self-discipline in this context is clearly the weighing of two good options and deciding of what is most important to you.

The Academic and Skilled

Students of knowledge and of skills must practice in order to become competent and to excel in their field or talent. Students must manage the competing goals of temporary enjoyment and long-term success. They must balance their time and energies such that they are able to complete the work and practice required by their studies with the rejuvenating activities of rest like watching television and hanging out with friends.

When one becomes greater than it ought, the student's studies suffer. If you are a student and you study to the exclusion of restful activities, your studies will decline in quality. However, if you participate in restful enjoyment too much, you will put yourself at risk of missing out on or not finishing your studying. Self-discipline, the management of conflicting goals, is highly relevant to this aspect of life.

The Professionally-Minded

Men and women in the professional world require a great deal of self-denial, self-control, and persistence as well. The demands of professional society are often great and call for both wisdom and the discipline to abide by the rules of the specific workplace.

Whether in the military, in which you need physical discipline to advance, or in a desk job where your mental and emotional energies and creativity are required, your hard work and continued effort are most often the basis of advancement.

The foundation of your success in the workforce often has something to do with self-discipline.

People in Relationships

As parents, spouses, friends, and children, we all have been in relationships with other people before. Often, we do not think about it, but relationships require self-discipline.

Interpersonal relationships are wily creatures and have all sorts of pitfalls and ways to go wrong. Self-discipline is not the only factor necessary for a good friendship or relationship, but it plays one of the vital roles in a relationship's stability.

Boundaries are the clearest way in which self-discipline plays a role: you must define what you will tolerate and what is intolerable and then abide by those limitations if a relationship is to maintain health. If you allow too much of the intolerable, you will become resentful of the other person, and the friendship might become spiteful.

Busy People and Anyone with Goals

In this day and age, when our lives seem busier than ever, self-discipline is essential to our survival and success. We must budget our time like we do our money and energies.

In addition, if you have any sort of long-term or even short-term goals, accomplishing them will take making a plan and sticking to it: in other words, it will take self-discipline. Through self-discipline, you can overcome the sense of pressure you feel and, instead of feeling overwhelmed, you will feel empowered to accomplish your goals.

Anyone Who Seeks to be Happy

American talk show host and best-selling author Dennis Prager tells us that *"happiness is dependent on self-discipline. We are the biggest obstacles to our own happiness. It is much easier to do battle with society and with others than to fight with our own nature."*

According to Prager, our happiness is dependent on our ability to deny ourselves on some level and on our ability to fight with our own nature. Self-discipline, therefore, is for everyone.

Action Steps

1. Which category discussed in this chapter do you resonate with the most?

2. How could self-discipline help you in that area?

CHAPTER 3: THE OBSTACLES TO SELF-DISCIPLINE

"What was it St. Augustine said? 'The mind commands the body and it obeys. The mind orders itself and meets resistance.'"

Frank Herbert in his novel, Dune

Key Takeaway: There are several factors working against us when it comes to self-discipline, including our tendency to be shortsighted, society's pressure to overindulgence and procrastination, and our own biology. However, these things CAN be overcome!

If self-discipline is so vital to our happiness and existence, why don't we practice it more often? Let's take a look at some reasons.

Ease of Giving into Temptations and Shortsightedness

To many of us, the long-term effects of a decision matter very little in relation to the short-term gain. Gary Ryan Blair, coach, motivator, and President of the GoalsGuy organization, puts it this way: *"Self-discipline is an act of cultivation. It requires you to connect today's actions to tomorrow's results. There's a season for sowing and a season for reaping. Self-discipline helps you know which is which."*

Too often, we are nearsighted in our view of the outcome of a choice we might make, thinking only of the immediate consequences and satisfaction we will receive, and not thinking of the long-term effect as just as vital and important. We need to rework our minds to think more about the more far-reaching effects of our decisions.

Indulgent Society of Procrastination

There is another reason that self-discipline is difficult for us: in the first world and perhaps in the world as a whole, society has become more permissive and even encouraging of indulgent behaviors. Overeating, extravagant spending, sexual promiscuity, and drunkenness have become not only commonplace but the norm for much of society, such that those who refrain from such practices are called prudish or fundamentalist. In addition, procrastination is almost bred into us from an early age, with society around us telling us that it is not only normal, but acceptable.

This phenomenon of overindulgence and procrastination discourages self-discipline simply by making a lack of discipline okay. We need to somehow surround ourselves with discipline if we are ever to find for ourselves the accountability to develop discipline.

Biological Pushback

Without getting too technical, there is another reason that self-discipline is difficult for us. There is a theory called "the energy model" that tells us that willpower, or the ability to be disciplined, is a depletable resource. That is, the more effort it takes to follow through on one commitment, the less willpower we will have available for the next task.

Now, whether the "energy" we need is food in the form of carbohydrates or dopamine in our brains is not proven, but the idea that self-control is in limited supply is a known fact.

We will talk about this more in a short bit, but for now, let it suffice to say that our very biology is working against us when it comes to self-discipline. What we need is to redefine the pathways in our brains that create the dopamine, a chemical causing us to feel happiness. By redefining happiness in this way, we will be able to successfully discipline ourselves to better decision-making and self-control.

We Do Not Know How

One other reason that we do not practice self-discipline, though likely not the last reason, is that we simply do not know how to implement it. Whether our parents were lax in their discipline of themselves and of us, or perhaps we chose as children and then as adults to ignore the importance of self-discipline because of the world in which we live, we have not learned the practical steps of becoming disciplined. We have not learned the "how-to's" of self-discipline, so even if the other factors above were irrelevant and we had the motivation to become disciplined, we would not know how to even start.

This does not make us stupid or unintelligent. It simply means we have not studied ourselves very well. We are so busy sometimes caring about performance for others, we forget to seek an understanding of ourselves: of our habits, our hang-ups, our weaknesses, and our strengths. We don't know what motivates us and was makes us feel dejected or defeated. We have little idea what makes us truly happy, and instead focus on our immediate pleasures. We do not look beyond the surface, oftentimes. However, we must look deeper into ourselves to see what we truly desire in life in order to make a plan to achieve what we want.

So…How?

We have taken a look at a number of things that keep us from what we desire most in life, which is most often obtained by self-discipline. I do not want to leave you in a state of defeat, however, after seeing this variety of factors that we must overcome.

Over the next few chapters, we will explore how to overcome the various things that impede our growth in self-discipline. Are you ready? Let's get to it!

Action Steps

1. Which obstacles play the biggest role in keeping you from practicing self-discipline in your life? How?

2. Have you studied your habits and hang-ups before?

3. What is the biggest lesson you have learned from failed attempts to improve your self-discipline?

CHAPTER 4: VISION, MOTIVATION, AND KNOWING WHY

"Self-discipline is self-caring."

M. Scott Peck

Key Takeaway: We must define our overall goal and keep our mind on it, or visualize it, if we are going to be successful. This might scare us, but in the end, we need to respect ourselves and our goals.

If we want to make ourselves happy or obtain what we want in life, we must become students of ourselves. *"Self-discipline is self-caring"*, according to M. Scott Peck, author of *The Road Less Traveled: A New Psychology of Love, Traditional Values and Spiritual Growth.*

Caring for ourselves means taking a good, long look at ourselves and making a plan to gift to ourselves the things that we most deeply desire. Caring for ourselves means having the self-discipline to say "No" to the things that put our hearts' desires in jeopardy. We must say "No" so that we can say "Yes" to the things we really do want, even if it means a bit of sacrifice in the short-term. We will be glad we have done so.

It is not enough just to want to be self-disciplined. We must have a measurable, long-term goal in mind to motivate us. This is true whether we want to be self-disciplined because we want to:

- control our emotions better
- attain a certain status or financial state
- complete a task like writing a book or win a competition, or
- any other variety of reasons.

We must define our goals first.

Defining Goals

Sometimes we shy away from defining our goals. We are afraid that defining them will doom us to failure, somehow. We become afraid that telling ourselves our goals will, in a way, jinx us to devastating inability to attain that goal. You might want to get married, or become an entrepreneur, or become the next best-selling author. I will tell you this: by not defining your goal, you are condemning yourself to failure already. By not taking the first steps to try to reach your dreams, you will never have a definition for self-discipline and your efforts will be shooting in the dark at a moving target.

Alternatively, we are afraid that defining our goals will bring us to the point of obtaining them, which is something that scares us. For example, you might want to become CEO of a company, but you are afraid to sit down and define that goal because, then, one day you would be the CEO of a company! You are afraid that you will not be able to live up to the position or persona you create for yourself. I suspect, though, that while you might not have the wisdom, knowledge and practicality to be made into a CEO tomorrow, if you choose to pursue such a thing and end up there, you will have grown to the point at which you are more than capable of such a thing.

Tony Robbins, arguably the world's most famous life and business coach, has a wonderful video on this topic that you can find on YouTube: 'How to END financial self-sabotage'.

He points out that, although at the surface level we may think we strive to attain financial wealth, at a deeper level we may be self-sabotage this goal without limiting beliefs. These limiting beliefs are often the result of what we were taught about money growing up (money doesn't grow on trees! Money can't buy happiness! Money is the root of all evil!). But we are not aware of that software running in the background, so to speak, slowing down the performance of our operating system. I very much encourage you to do the exercise in this video, by answering all the questions. I am 100% certain that what you will uncover will be mind-blowing...

Getting back to the point: you need a goal to really reap the benefits of practicing self-discipline. Self-discipline is something that is individual to each person and will look different for each person. Therefore, you must define what self-control is (what you are keeping yourself from) and what persistence is (what you are pursuing). Self-discipline for the sake of self-discipline is miserable, because you are not desiring of its reward. Self-discipline for the sake of a cause or goal will make you unstoppable.

Keeping the Goal in Mind

Another thing that is helpful in developing self-discipline in terms of defining your goals is to remind yourself daily of your purpose and intentions. Write your overall goal on a sticky note, and put it on the mirror in your bathroom. Take a picture of it to hang on your wall. Or find a song that represents your desires and play it every morning. Whatever works for you!

This is not intended to make you live so much in the future that you do not enjoy the present, but it is intended to help you think about what you can do today to push yourself one step closer to your goals.

Respect Yourself

Another important reminder is to respect yourself and your goals. As actor Clint Eastwood put it, *"Respect your efforts, respect yourself. Self-respect leads to self-discipline. When you have both firmly under your belt, that's real power."*

You must respect your own goals and not think of them too lowly or too highly. We must not put ourselves down by comparing to others and to their goals and accomplishments.

We need to know ourselves and what makes us tick, such that we can pursue the things that make us happy, not what makes other people happy.

As Eastwood lets us know, self-respect leads to self-discipline because it takes what we love and allows us to truly love it, without shame and without apology. With love, discipline comes more easily.

Action Steps

1. What are your goals? If you haven't set your goals, take out a piece of paper and write them down, but long-term and short-term goals.
2. What can you do daily to remind yourself of your goal? Is there a song that reminds you of it, and, if so, which song? Can you draw a picture, write a note, etc.?
3. Watch the video 'How to END financial self-sabotage' on YouTube.

CHAPTER 5: SET MEASURABLE GOALS

"The more specific and measurable your goal, the more quickly you will be able to identify, locate, create, and implement the use of the necessary resources for its achievement."

Charles J. Givens

Key Takeaway: We have to split our goal up into measurable, achievable pieces. Then, we must take note of what works and what does not work by recording our successes and failures, which will allow us to plan more intelligently the next time.

Self-discipline is dependent upon having measurable goals. Splitting a goal into smaller, more achievable tasks is often a good idea and will increase your ability to be self-disciplined. If you have smaller goals within a larger objective, you will find that everything feels less overwhelming and more possible.

Lists

Lists are one way to split the goal up into tasks. If you cannot split the goal up into a list of steps, it might be just as good to estimate the number of hours you might spend on the project and schedule time within each week or day to work on it. With these lists, you can even make sublists to be more organized and help break the tasks down into even more manageable chunks.

How about an example?

Clean the House

- **Clean the kitchen (TOTAL: 2 hours)**
    - Wash the dishes (1 hour)
    - Clean the sink (15 minutes)
    - Wipe off the counters (15 minutes)
    - Clean the refrigerator (30 minutes)

- **Clean the bathroom (TOTAL: 1 hour 10 minutes)**
    - Scrub the shower (30 minutes)
    - Scrub the toilet (10 minutes)
    - Wipe off the sink (15 minutes)

- o Clean the mirror (15 minutes)

- **Clean the living room (TOTAL: 1 hour 30 minutes)**
  - o Pick up the objects scattered about (30 minutes)
  - o Dust (20 minutes)
  - o Vacuum (40 minutes)
  - o Etc.

Writing down how much time you approximate the task will take is a good practice, because it gives you an idea of when the task might fit in your day or week and helps you feel that there is an end in sight instead of an ambiguous question mark of a time frame. This brings us to the planning stage.

Planning – Plan Regularly

Planning takes your list and makes you accountable to finishing it. Whether you buy a paper planner or you use smartphone and computer apps like Google Calendar, ToodleDo, HabitRPG etc., you will need a way to keep track of activities that you plan to do and keep a record of what you have accomplished. This planner can even take the form of a simple piece of paper with a list for each day of the week, such that you switch the paper out every week. However, with most goals of self-discipline, your goal will take longer than a week to accomplish, and so you will likely want a more robust planning tool than one sheet of paper for a week.

When you plan, a good rule of thumb that I have learned is to plan one bigger, **productive** task for in the **morning** and one bigger, productive thing for in the **afternoon**, as well one **fun** task in the **morning** and one fun thing in the **afternoon**.

You can certainly accomplish more if you are feeling up to it, but planning two of these two types of activities each day ensures that, at the end of the day, you will be able to look back and see the specific ways in which you were self-disciplined that day. This will motivate you going forward to do the same thing again, and after a while, you can try adding in more productivity or movement toward your overall goals.

Make sure to look ahead as well. Plan the short-term, of course, the next week or so at a time, and make sure you also have a rough sketch of what the more long-range plans are as well.

Finally, make sure to plan regularly. Block out a time every week or every month for a half hour or so to write in your planner. Think of it as a place to make the rough outlines of your dreams coming to fruition. This is exciting! You are writing down your future successes and victories! This is no mere planning session, this is dreaming in action and should be a time of inspiration that motivates you to move forward toward your goals.

Measure Success and Failure – Plan Accordingly

With your plan, in your planner or on the app in which you choose to record your progress, make sure that you have a way to look back and measure your success and failure. This is not to make you feel bad about yourself. It is not negative reinforcement. Instead, it is a way to look at your patterns and learn to plan more effectively.

Perhaps you find that you do not do well when you schedule exercise for in the afternoon. Or you find that, in the morning, you have a higher success rate with making phone calls in your position with your company.

Whatever the case, make sure to listen to your successes and failures and plan accordingly. Do not plan exercise as an afternoon activity. Instead, try planning it as one of your first activities of the day. Make sure that, once you arrive at work, you check your voicemails to return calls in the morning and make your phone calls for the day in that window. Your successes and failures are not the measure of your worth but an indication of how you work best.

Give Yourself Check-In Points

Especially when you are quitting an activity or habit, you need to have an endpoint and check-in point in mind. For example, if you want to quit smoking as your act of self-discipline, it is overwhelming to think you will NEVER again smoke a cigarette. The word, "never," paralyzes your will and ability to follow through on your commitment. It becomes easier and easier to say, "well, after this last one," or "I'll start tomorrow." However, if you tell yourself you will refrain from smoking, drinking, eating unhealthy foods, or drinking soda for a week or a month at most, you will be better able to restrain yourself.

I have mostly been eating vegetarian for the last couple of years. However, I don't call myself a vegetarian. Why not? Because that would imply that I can *never* eat meat. And that would make it so difficult! Especially in the beginning.

Remember what we discussed earlier, that willpower is a depletable resource? So, what I do is that I allow myself to eat meat when I *really* crave it. Or when I just don't want to be that one person in the room at Thanksgiving or Christmas that can't eat that turkey. Because I allow myself that leniency, 99% of my meals are vegetarian. And I don't beat myself up or feel guilty when I eat meat that 1% of the time. The longer I do this, the easier it becomes. It's the new normal.

Behavioral economist, David Goldstein said, "*I think self-discipline is something, it's like a muscle. The more you exercise it, the stronger it gets.*" If you build your muscles of self-restraint and self-denial in short spurts and recommit to another week or month at the end of the first week or month, and you continue to do so indefinitely, you will find yourself loving the freedom you obtain more than the addiction that was enslaving you. And not long after, clean air and healthy lungs will matter more to you than the cigarette. Soon, you will crave vegetables and fruits and lean meats instead of sugars and simple starches. And water will be more refreshing to you than a soda.

Action Steps

1. For each of your goals, write down the steps you need to take to achieve them. Where possible, make sure these steps are measurable, so you can track your progress.

2. Create check-in points along the way to achieving your goals. Whenever you reach such a milestone, ask yourself: how did I get here? Do I need to change my course to stay on track to achieving my goal?

CHAPTER 6: BE ACCOUNTABLE

"Maybe you're not perfect, but you're willing to actually look at yourself and take some kind of accountability. That's a change. It might not mean you can turn everything around, but I think there's something incredibly hopeful about that."

Brie Larson

Key Takeaway: *Writing things in a planner or recording them in a productivity app will help immensely with accountability. If this ever overwhelms you, fall back on an accountability partner and remind yourself of your role models in order to remember your ultimate goals.*

American actress Brie Larson tells us that there is something hopeful in the choice you can make to be accountable. Indeed, in terms of self-discipline, *"The road to character is built by confronting your own weakness,"* according to New York Times writer David Brooks. It is dangerous to go alone, though, in confronting your shortcomings, so you must have some tools to take with you. We will now take a look at some of those tools.

Planners and Productivity Apps – Tracking the Measurable Goals

We discussed earlier creating measurable goals that you can track on paper or in a computer or smartphone app. This is vital to your success in self-discipline. Creating measurable goals helps you to not feel overwhelmed, and tracking them makes you accountable to following through. It could be as simple as creating a daily check box in a planner or app.

Most productivity apps give you the ability to track habits and daily goals. ToodleDo for example, a paid app with a free version, allows you to record hours worked on a project, check boxes for a habit, number of times per day that you did or failed to do something, etc., and then it creates graphs to look back at your month to measure your successes and failures.

If you are a technologically-inclined person, I would recommend considering the free and paid productivity apps that are compatible with your smartphone. This will allow you the greatest access to your productivity tools and make the excuse that, "I didn't feel like turning on my computer" obsolete.

If you are more of a pen-and-paper person, there are a multitude of helpful planners that have come out in the past few years to help with planning and productivity:

- Panda Planner
- Passion Planner
- Erin Condren planners
- Day Designer, and
- Franklin Covey planners

are all examples of more robust planners than a simple monthly or weekly planner.

Try a few options and see which one works best for you! Set a time each week for planning and evaluating the previous week in terms of your self-discipline. You will not improve if you do not know what is working and what is not working.

Accountability Partners

We talked earlier about the way that society commends and even pressures us to indulgence and lack of self-discipline. We can overcome this hurdle by choosing friends and family to keep us accountable. What does this mean, though, for a friend or family member to hold us accountable?

This means that we will confide in the accountability partner our shortcomings as well as our desire to become self-disciplined in a specific area of life.

Choosing an Accountability Partner

First, we must ensure that the person we are trusting with our accountability is trustworthy for the task. They must be self-disciplined at some level, but not necessarily in the same area of self-discipline that we are seeking to teach ourselves. (Such a person would be a role model, and we will talk about them in the next section of this chapter. Role models can also make good accountability partners but are not necessary to the role.)

Instead, the self-discipline that an accountability partner must exemplify is in social boundaries and courage to speak the truth: that is, an accountability partner must be able to tell you the hard truth sometimes, in a compassionate way, to help motivate you to the desired behavior you are pursuing.

They must be supportive of your cause as well. It is for this reason that a smoker might not be the best person to be your accountability partner to stop smoking cigarettes. They likely would not see the need or would have mixed feelings about your goal, and so you would be better off seeking out someone who sees the health value of not smoking and who can remind you of this without being hypocritical.

Meeting with an Accountability Partner

You might choose an accountability partner whom you see often on an informal basis, like a good friend or family member. This might be an ideal choice because they can see your progress firsthand. They will also see your failure and be able to gently remind you of your goals and desire for self-discipline.

Alternatively, you might choose someone who is not a close friend but more of an acquaintance, such as a therapist or counselor, to be part of your accountability.

This would allow the accountability partner less fear in pointing out your shortcomings that week or month, since they do not feel a friendship is hanging in the balance if they offend you. However, this will also depend on your devotion to being honest with this person, as they can only be as helpful as you are truthful.

Role Models

Another helpful form of accountability is to have role models that you study and imitate. This might be someone in your life, a public figure, or a historical person about whom you can learn through reading. Having more than one role model might also be helpful.

Choosing a Role Model

When you think of your goal, who in your life or of whom you know best exemplifies that trait, habit, persona, or position? Of whom do you think when you imagine success in the area of self-discipline that you are pursuing?
The person that comes to mind would be your "role model." Choose with care, because who you model is may determine who you might become. When you think of this person, are

they someone you respect? Are they someone you would not mind becoming?

Learning About Your Role Model

Once you choose your role model, you will need to learn about them. You will want to learn:

- the influences in their life
- their motivations
- their successes
- their failures, as well as
- about the people that molded them and about their role models.

These things will give you a picture of their life and the factors motivating them as well as the things hindering them from their ultimate success.

If the person is living and you can talk to them directly, this task might be easier, as you will be able to ask them the questions in person. However, if this role model is an inaccessible public figure or a historical figure, your job is not a great deal more difficult: you will simply need to read about the person. You can read interviews, biographies, autobiographies, and even the written works, both fiction and nonfiction, of the person.

Letting Your Role Models Influence You

This is all well and good, but how do your role models help you stay accountable? First, you will want to draw comparisons and contrasts between the information you gather about the person and your own life. What influences are similar in your life to what has influenced their outlook and motives? What influences are different? What were their motivations and how are your motivations different from or parallel to theirs?

Second, you will want to remind yourself on a regular basis about this person's successes and how you foresee yourself in a similar position. This interlocks with the daily reminder you have for yourself in the form of a song, a note, a painting, etc. about your goals. This will recharge your willpower to self-discipline.

Action Steps

1. Spend an hour researching the many different productivity apps that are available for your computer and smartphone. Install the ones you like and start experimenting with them for at least a week (Why? Because it may take some time to get used to them).

2. Find an accountability partner. Who are some people that can hold you accountable to achieving self-discipline and your goals?

3. Pick a self-discipline role model. Whose successes (and failures!) inspire you to hustle and achieve your goals?

CHAPTER 7: HOW TO RESIST TEMPTATIONS

"The biggest human temptation is to settle for too little."

Thomas Merton

Key Takeaway: We should remind ourselves of the positive outcome of self-discipline rather than scare ourselves with "what-if's". Additionally, we need to replace any negative habit or activity with something we enjoy that is good for us. We can do this through a reward system. When possible, we need to avoid tempting situations and not put ourselves at risk.

Temptations are bound to grip us when we decide to pursue self-discipline. We are condemned to give in to these temptations unless we make an informed and concerted effort to resist them. Resistance usually is some form of avoidance when it comes to temptation: putting ourselves in a position where we will not face temptation rather than trying to actively resist a temptation once it comes upon us. There are a few ways we can avoid temptation, which we will now discuss.

Positive Reinforcement

If you find self-criticism does not motivate you, you are not alone. Many people find that negation and critical self-talk paralyze them in terms of making the correct decision going forward, giving them visions of disaster that they want to avoid, instead of dreams of success they want to target. You are not alone in desiring positive reinforcement rather than self-critique as the main motivator for your pursuit of self-discipline.

Criticism and negative self-talk are based on fear as a motivator rather than love or hope. Author and revered thinker, Ayn Rand, has some powerful things to say about this:

"It is not death we wish to avoid, but life that we wish to live. You, who have lost the concept of the difference, you who claim that fear and joy are incentives of **equal power** *– and secretly add that fear is the more 'practical' – you do not wish to live, and only fear of death holds you to the existence you have damned."*

She adds, *"Achieving life is not the equivalent of avoiding death. Joy is not the absence of pain."*

These are some strong words from a strong woman of discipline. What she is saying is that our pursuit of good things should not be because we simply want to avoid what is bad. Relating to our topic at hand, self-discipline is not for the sake of avoiding ill-feeling and discomfort, but for the sake of finding happiness and joy. Self-discipline is to provide hope, not just negate fear and anxiety.

Thomas Merton, a modern, Catholic theologian, wrote that the temptation that besets us most often is the temptation to settle for too little. Instead of thinking of how giving into the temptation would negatively affect us, which would use fear to compel us to self-discipline, why do we not think of what positive results would come from choosing the disciplined option? Instead of thinking of how poor we will be after the spending spree on which we are tempted to embark, why not think of the satisfaction of saving up for that car or house we have always wanted?

Replace Negatives with Positives

As humans, we are not creatures that do well with a void. What I mean by this is: if we decide to stop a certain habit or activity, we do not do well with the boredom that comes during the time the habit or activity used to fill. If we decide to stop gambling online, for example, but do not replace that activity with something else, boredom creeps in as we sit idly, and we are tempted to resume the activity that we are trying so hard to avoid. Self-discipline requires both a negative and a positive force, such that when you stop one thing, you must start another, better thing to replace it.

Doing this will help you to avoid temptation by refocusing your mind's energies on another task. Instead of thinking about drinking alcohol at night, try going to a coffee shop and meeting new people, or bring a friend along and share stories over a coffee drink (decaffeinated if need be). Instead of eating that piece of chocolate cake, make yourself a salad with some sweet dressing and eat that, putting the cake out of sight. There are many examples we could make of how to replace old bad habits with new good habits. What are some good habits with which you would like to replace your bad habits? Make a list of possibilities, so that, if you do not feel like participating in one activity, you have a choice of other, positive activities in which you might take part.

Reward Systems

One more specific way to replace a negative with a positive and to positively reinforce a behavior or pattern is to create a reward system for yourself. This reward system should allow you to gift certain items or activities to yourself based on how well you perform a task of self-discipline. This brings up a few questions.

What Kind of Rewards?

The rewards should not be related to what you are attempting to avoid. For example, if you are avoiding spending money, the reward for not spending money should not be something you purchase. Instead, you might choose something like an afternoon reading in the park or taking a hot bath. This will help you avoid the trap of trade-offs: "Well if I don't spend money on that reward, I could buy this instead, and of course then I would not receive the reward because I will have spent the money on something else, but it was going to be spent either way."

The same goes for:

- dieting (no food-related rewards)
- addictions (no addiction-related allowances)
- exercise (no days off from exercise when you would otherwise be exercising)
- etc.

Choose a reward that is special and motivates you: something you want but do not often allow yourself to have.

How Often Should I Give Myself Rewards?

Choose small goals that can be accomplished once a week or so. Then make sure the reward is something you would still look forward to after a week. Daily rewards start to lose their savor and rewards that take longer than a week to reach often seem a bit unreachable in the short-term.

What Amount of Success Should Be My Aim?

Do not aim for 100% success at first. Somewhere between 75% and 90% should be the goal ass you start out. It might be good to have a tiered reward system, if you feel like taking that much time to create one. For example, if you write a list of things you want to accomplish around the house, you could say that the rewards are:

- 50% accomplished – a nice bath
- 60% accomplished – some fancy chocolate
- 70% accomplished – a new book
- 80% accomplished – a new DVD
- 90% accomplished – a stroll in the park and all of the above
- 100% accomplished – invite friends to watch the DVD and enjoy all of the above

These rewards will help you avoid feeling like a failure if you do not get done with everything on your list, but they will also motivate you to try to finish as much as you can. Think of some rewards that would help motivate you.

Avoid Tempting Situations

A problem we often encounter as we are attempting to develop self-discipline is that we do not know our limits. We think, "I can just window shop, I will not buy anything because I do not have anything in particular I want right now." Or we think, "I'll go to that fancy, new, Italian restaurant with all the desserts and just order a salad for my diet." We think that because we are not interested in a temptation at the moment in which we choose to participate in an activity, that temptation will not overcome us once we do engage in that activity.

Whether we are attempting to stop drinking alcohol, or we want to save up for a down payment on a house, or we have any other goal that requires self-discipline, we must learn not to engage in activities that bring us near our temptations, as far as it is within our power. If we do not want to drink, let's not go to a party where drinking will surround us. If we don't want to spend money, don't window shop, neither in a store or online. One of the easiest but least utilized aspects of self-discipline is stopping temptation before it starts.

Action Steps

1. What are the biggest temptations preventing you from achieving your goal(s)? Write them down. Just putting them on a piece of paper can already be very insightful.

2. How can you avoid these temptations?

3. Create a list of rewards to motivate you to stay disciplined. What are some rewards you would enjoy for achieving your goals? Do not only reward yourself for achieving a goal (like writing a book), but also for reaching milestones along the way (like finishing a chapter).

CHAPTER 8: WHAT IF I FAIL?

"Success is not final, failure is not fatal; it is the courage to continue that counts."

Winston Churchill

Key Takeaway: *We must remember that failure is normal and to be expected. We must seek forgiveness from ourselves and others when we fail. Writing down our list of gratitudes will help us refocus and be thankful. We must reorganize and regroup with our support network when we fail so that we can persist in our efforts and try, try again. Finally, we need to try to get regular sleeping and eating patterns in place in order to maintain our willpower.*

If you seek to become self-disciplined, you will fail. Over and over again, you will fail. You will pick up that cigarette, you will scream at your children, you will eat that piece of cake, you will fail that test because you did not study enough, you will eat a hamburger while fasting from meat for Lent, and you will fail to do what you committed to do, over and over again. It will not be as often as you imagined, seeing as we are often far more capable than we hoped, but even one failure is more than we wanted.

The key to success is courage to continue, according to Winston Churchill in the quote at the beginning of the chapter. The object of our victory in self-discipline is not lack of failure but the filling of our lives with so many successes that the failures do not matter anymore. Succeed, succeed, and succeed again, and when you fail, do not let the failure be your final act. Get up, dust yourself off, and keep trying.

This all sounds great, but practically speaking, how do we find the courage to continue despite failures, multiple failures even? Following are some tips to help guide you through failure to success.

Forgiveness and Humility

Forgiveness is vital to your success. You must accept forgiveness for your mistakes if you are ever to move past them. Your failure affects more than just you, but, if you surround yourself with good, caring, gracious people, they will forgive you and encourage you to move forward. You must be willing to humble yourself to accept their forgiveness.

How does this work? If you are addicted to a substance or behavior, your support network or friends and family will hurt every time you return to that addiction, even if you just return to it for a moment. This is because they care about you and want to see you succeed. You must accept their love and grace in order to move out of the ditch of self-pity that we often dig for ourselves when we have failed.

Self-discipline requires us to humble ourselves under the yoke of humanity. We are not gods. We are not capable of every good thing or even everything that we ever want to accomplish. However, we doom ourselves to utter defeat in every area of life if we choose to sit in self-pity rather than in humility.

Gratitude

One of the most important acts of self-discipline we can accomplish is rather simple, and even easy at times. It is gratitude. Making a list every day of the things for which we are grateful helps our minds think positively. It reminds us that, even without the self-discipline and object of our goals, we are fortunate in many ways. I would recommend buying a small notebook and recording your daily gratitude list.

You might find that some things are repeated often or that your lists become longer as time goes on. This is a good thing. It means that you are remembering the things that give you joy in life, and the longer the lists get, the more mindful you are of the things that make your life easier, happier, and more successful.

This will in turn help you to work on your self-discipline without clinging to it as the only source of happiness. The reason you do not want self-discipline to be your only source of joy is because it can fail. We are human, and we make mistakes. If your self-discipline is the only thing defining your joyfulness in life, you are bound to be disappointed, even devastated. This will only serve to instill fear as a motivation, which, as we discussed in the previous chapter, will cause you more trouble than it helps.

Reorganizing and Regrouping

When you fail, it might be in such a way that your work planning for the next few weeks is made obsolete. This is okay. You will fail sometimes, and very miserably, such that an entire week's worth of activities must be moved to the following week.

The most important thing to do in such a case is to reorganize. You will need to block out a half hour to an hour to reevaluate what needs to be done, what you can stand to not finish, and what can be finished at a later date. Then, you will need to write down the changes in your planner or record them in your productivity app on the computer or on your smartphone.

Another very important step in the process is to regroup, which means talking to your support network of accountability partners. You will need to let them know what has occurred and possibly would benefit from telling them the reason that caused the failure. Then, you need to allow yourself to be encouraged by them to start afresh.

Persistence

Thomas Edison is famous for having tried thousands of materials as possible filaments for the light bulb before finally finding that carbonized thread did the trick. Remarking upon his failed experiments, he said: *"I have not failed. I've just found 10,000 ways that won't work."*

We must cultivate the same mindset in ourselves in terms of self-discipline: persistence derived from an experimental mindset. We have not failed to break our habits, but instead we have found another method that is not working quite correctly. When we fail, we simply jot down the observation in our notebook and move forward with another method or with the same method in a new mindset.

Sleep and Eat Regularly

We must sleep and eat regularly to maintain mental and emotional energy if we are to attempt anything requiring self-discipline. Sleep deprivation is a commonly-used torture method to wear down willpower to resist temptation. Knowing this, why would we ever allow ourselves to miss out on sleep when it is within our power to ensure ourselves adequate rest? Knowing that sleep is essential to our pursuit of self-discipline, one of our objects of discipline might become to go to sleep by a certain time each night.

In addition, irregular eating patterns can negatively affect our sense of motivation and our ability to overcome temptation. In other words, regular eating patterns are necessary for self-discipline. This is not to say you must go on a diet of any sort, only that you should eat a regular three to five normal- to small-sized meals per day at regular intervals. This will help keep up your mental and emotional energy to maintain self-discipline.

Action Steps

1. Understand that anyone who is successful at anything, has failed countless times before reaching that success.
2. Reflect on this, with your eyes closed: how can you be kind and forgiving with yourself, when you fail?
3. Every morning after waking up, and every evening before going to bed, write down three things that you are grateful for. This does wonders for your mindset!
4. When you fail at something, take a step back to reorganize. Do you need to change your priorities? What could you have done differently?

5. Do you sleep and eat regularly? Are you willing to commit to building better habits in these areas as part of your self-discipline regimen?

CHAPTER 9: FINAL THOUGHTS

Wow, that went fast, didn't it? We've come to the end of this book, *Self-Discipline Master*.

You should now have a good understanding of self-discipline and be able to create goals and make plans to achieve them, hold yourself accountable and motivate yourself, fight temptation, and overcome failure to continue in the pursuit of your dreams.

To wrap up our journey in learning about self-discipline, I want to give you a practical list to go through to start your self-discipline process by summarizing the book in bullet point form.

Your To-Do List

The following list is comprehensive of what we have discussed throughout this book.

You might focus your energies on some steps and not others, or you might try to go through each step very carefully. Do not worry: it is the trying that counts and that will propel you toward self-discipline. See what works for you!

Vision, Motivation and Knowing Why

- Define your goals.
- Determine how you will keep your goal in mind and implement it.

Measurable Goals

- Create a list of steps to making you succeed at this goal.
- Obtain a planner or productivity app.
- Design rough outline and the first week of your self-discipline regimen.
- Measure successes and failures within the first week.
- Create check-in points to check-in on your progress later. (1 week, 1 month, 3 months, etc.)

Be Accountable

- Make sure your planner/productivity app is going to work for what you need it to do.

- Determine who you will ask to be accountability partners.
- Ask them! Inform them of your struggle and your goals.
- Determine who are your role models.
- If accessible in person: set up a meeting with them and prepare questions about their motivations, struggles, background and goals.
- If NOT accessible in person: Determine what resources you will need to learn about this person and obtain those resources. Then spend some time reading and studying those resources, answering the questions of their motivations, struggles, background and goals.

Obstacles to Self-Discipline

- Determine your temptations in terms of the particular goal of self-discipline that you have.
- Determine who you need to stay away from and who you need to be around with your goal in mind. Who supports you in your self-discipline and who encourages you to just forget it?

- Read books, like this one, and refer to them regularly when trying to figure out how to go about developing self-discipline.

How To Resist Temptations?

- Determine what positive reinforcement will motivate you to look at the object of your self-discipline with love and not fear.
- If you are refraining from a habit or activity, determine what you will replace it with.
- Figure out what rewards will motivate you and create a list or tiered list of rewards for accomplishing your goals.
- Determine who you will need to limit your time with and who you will need to be around more often to encourage you. Figure out which activities cause you temptation and plan other things in their place.

What If I fail?

- Ask forgiveness of yourself and others when you make a mistake, and accept their forgiveness.

- Obtain a journal for writing down your list of gratitudes. Write in it every day, even if it is a short list of one or two things.
- When you fail, sit down and take time to reorganize your plan.
- When you fail, take time to tell your accountability partners and let them encourage you to get back up.
- Remember to see your self-discipline journey as an experiment – you are just figuring out what works and what does not work.
- Sleep and eat regularly.

Now Get Out There And Do It!

With these closing comments, I would like to encourage you in your pursuit of self-discipline.

Whether you are starting out as a discipline pro or just taking your first steps in self-discipline, the journey to leading a disciplined lifestyle will be a lifelong endeavor. You will never entirely "arrive" because every moment you have the choice whether or not you will exercise self-discipline in the next moment.

That being said, I encourage you to enjoy the journey. Self-discipline will allow you to pursue your dreams with more traction underfoot, and you will find yourself more successful in your goals. However, do not forget to enjoy what you have right now while you pursue what you might receive.

And remember, you are not alone in this! You have a whole multitude of people who are pursuing self-discipline in their own way. If you have gained anything from this book, perhaps you can share what you have learned with others.

All the best to you in your pursuits!

RESOURCES

Planners

- **Day Designer** – daily/weekly/monthly, customizable art, goal setting worksheets
- **Erin Condren Planners** – weekly/monthly, customizable layout and art, hardbound and spiral-bound
- **Panda Planner** – daily/weekly/monthly, daily prioritizing tools
- **Passion Planner** – weekly/monthly, undated planner available, motivation/reflection pages
- **Plum Paper** – weekly/monthly, extremely customizable layout
- **Rituals for Living Dreambook** – weekly/monthly OR purely goal setting, motivational worksheets

Productivity Apps

- **Any.do** – Android/iOS/web, calendar, to do list, integrates with other apps, free & Premium
- **HabitRPG** – Android/iOS/web, habits & tasks, accountability, "Gamify your life," free & fun
- **KanbanFlow** – Android/iOS/web, free and Premium, robust organization of tasks
- **Nozbe** – all platforms (including Linux), free and Premium, integrates with other apps
- **OmniFocus** – Apple, many ways to look at tasks, integrates to various Apple platforms
- **Todoist** – all platforms, free and Premium, distraction-free design, organize tasks and goals
- **Toodledo** – Android/iOS/web, many analytical tools, task, habits, lists, notes, free and Premium
- **Trello** – Android/iOS/web, free and Premium, collaborative
- **Week Plan** – Apple/Android/web/Windows, free and Premium, analytics tools (with Premium)
- **Wunderlist** – all platforms (including Kindle Fire), lots of features, sync across devices

ACTION STEPS RECAP

Here's a recap of all the action steps. In one place. If you haven't taken any action yet, do it now!

Chapter 1: What is Self-Discipline, And Why Should You Care?

1. How do you define self-discipline?
2. In what areas do you demonstrate good self-discipline?
3. In what areas are you lacking self-discipline?
4. Mimic the Marshmallow experiment. Buy something sweet you really like. Put it in front of you, as you sit quietly in a room. Don't touch it. Instead, imagine being 4 years old again. What is going through your head? Can you delay the gratification of eating that yumminess that's staring you in the face?

Chapter 2: Who Needs Self-Discipline?

1. Which category discussed in this chapter do you resonate with the most?
2. How could self-discipline help you in that area?

Chapter 3: The Obstacles To Self-Discipline

1. Which obstacles play the biggest role in keeping you from practicing self-discipline in your life? How?
2. Have you studied your habits and hang-ups before?
3. What is the biggest lesson you have learned from failed attempts to improve your self-discipline?

Chapter 4: Vision, Motivation, And Knowing Why

1. What are your goals? If you haven't set your goals, take out a piece of paper and write them down, but long-term and short-term goals.
2. What can you do daily to remind yourself of your goal? Is there a song that reminds you of it, and, if so, which song? Can you draw a picture, write a note, etc.?
3. Watch the video 'How to END financial self-sabotage' on YouTube.

Chapter 5: Set Measurable Goals

1. For each of your goals, write down the steps you need to take to achieve them. Where possible, make sure

these steps are measurable, so you can track your progress.

2. Create check-in points along the way to achieving your goals. Whenever you reach such a milestone, ask yourself: how did I get here? Do I need to change my course to stay on track to achieving my goal?

Chapter 6: Be Accountable

1. Spend an hour researching the many different productivity apps that are available for your computer and smartphone. Install the ones you like and start experimenting with them for at least a week (Why? Because it may take some time to get used to them).

2. Find an accountability partner. Who are some people that can hold you accountable to achieving self-discipline and your goals?

3. Pick a self-discipline role model. Whose successes (and failures!) inspire you to hustle and achieve your goals?

Chapter 7: How To Resist Temptations

1. What are the biggest temptations preventing you from achieving your goal(s)? Write them down. Just putting them on a piece of paper can already be very insightful.

2. How can you avoid these temptations?

3. Create a list of rewards to motivate you to stay disciplined. What are some rewards you would enjoy for achieving your goals? Do not only reward yourself for achieving a goal (like writing a book), but also for reaching milestones along the way (like finishing a chapter).

Chapter 8: What If I Fail?

1. Understand that anyone who is successful at anything, has failed countless times before reaching that success.

2. Reflect on this, with your eyes closed: how can you be kind and forgiving with yourself, when you fail?

3. Every morning after waking up, and every evening before going to bed, write down three things that you are grateful for. This does wonders for your mindset!

4. When you fail at something, take a step back to reorganize. Do you need to change your priorities? What could you have done differently?

5. Do you sleep and eat regularly? Are you willing to commit to building better habits in these areas as part of your self-discipline regimen?

DID YOU LIKE THIS BOOK?

If you enjoyed this book, I would like to ask you for a favor. Please leave a review on Amazon!

Reviews are the lifeblood of independent authors. I know, you're short on time. But I would really appreciate even just a few sentences!

To leave a review, you can search for *Self-Discipline Master* on Amazon and click 'Write a customer review'.

Your voice is important for this book to reach as many people as possible.

The more reviews this book gets, the more people will be able to find it and learn how they can become more disciplined, too.

IF YOU DID NOT LIKE THIS BOOK, THEN PLEASE TELL ME! You can email me at feedback@semsoli.com, to share with me what you did not like. Perhaps I can change it.

A book does not have to be stagnant, in today's world. With feedback from readers like yourself, I can improve the book. So, you can impact the quality of this book, and I welcome your feedback. Help make this book better for everyone!

Thank you again for reading this book and good luck with applying everything you have learned!

I'm rooting for you…

NOTES

Made in the USA
Middletown, DE
23 January 2019